G000253631

A BOOT UP

THE MENDIPS

Rodney Legg

First published in Great Britain in 2009

British Library Cataloguing-in-Publication Data
A CIP record for this title is available from the British Library

ISBN 978 1 906887 10 0

PiXZ Books
Halsgrove House, Ryelands Industrial Estate,
Bagley Road, Wellington, Somerset TA21 9PZ
Tel: 01823 653777
Fax: 01823 216796
email: sales@halsgrove.com

An imprint of Halstar Ltd, part of the Halsgrove group of companies
Information on all Halsgrove titles is available at: www.halsgrove.com

Printed and bound by Grafiche Flaminia, Italy

Contents

How to use this book

The Area

The Mendips as it is colloquially known - correctly it is simply non-plural Mendip - lies between the Somerset Levels and Bristol's immediate countryside on the English side of the Bristol Channel. The Mendip Hills are an escarpment of carboniferous limestone, dating from 330 million years ago in the Coal Age, which was uplifted by a collision of the Earth's tectonic plates into a plateau at around 1,000 feet above present sea level.

It provides excellent walking country, generally with firm and well defined paths that offer sweeping views. Our coverage here is from west to east.

Under your feet is a rich archaeological heritage from the Palaeolithic through to Anglo-Saxon times, plus numerous caverns, gorges and holes where past and present river systems have dissolved their way underground. Rich seams of lead and silver have been extracted over the past 2,000 years.

The Routes

All routes are circular - meaning they bring you back to the starting point - and are of moderate length. They vary from four to eight miles and are graded from one to three boots - from easy to the more challenging. They are ideal for families or groups of friends looking for an afternoon in glorious historic countryside or for a more leisurely walk with a suitable pause at a pub or refreshment spot en route. None of the terrain is pushchair friendly, so back-pack the toddler.

Starting points are given with map references and postcodes, because the latter are necessary for some car-borne navigation systems, including that used by an ambulance crew who told me they were 15 minutes late in arriving at an emergency because no postcode was given.

Direction details specify compass points which, clockwise, are N (north), NNE (north-northeast), E (east), ESE (east-southeast), SE (south-east), SSE (south-southeast), S (south), SSW (south-southwest), SW (south-west), WSW (west-southwest), W (west), WNW (west-northwest), NW (north-west) and WNW (west-northwest). The general direction can be assumed to remain the same until another compass point is given. Carry a compass.

Routes are along public rights of way or across access land. Both categories may be subject to change or diversion. Remember that conditions under foot will vary greatly according to the season and the weather. Do not set off into the hills if fog is present or likely.

Parking spaces are specified on the assumption that many walkers will arrive by car or bicycle. Where public transport is mentioned, there were options currently available, but check these with the provider before setting off and always make sure you also know the time of the last bus or train.

The Maps

Though we give a self-contained potted description of each walk you may need a map or global positioning system to find its parking pint. Our sketch maps can only be a rough guide. A detailed map will prove useful if you stray from the route or are forced to cut the walk short. Remember that practical difficulties on the day may range from exhaustion to hill fog.

Three large-scale Ordnance Survey maps currently cover the Mendip Hills. These are Explorer 153 (Weston-super-Mare), 141 (Glastonbury, Wells) and 142 (Shepton Mallet, Frome). For availability, access www.ordnancesurvey.co.uk/leisure.

Key to Symbols Used

Level of difficulty:

Easy 🍃

Fair 🍃 🍃

More challenging 🍃 🍃 🍃

Map symbols:

🚗 Park & start

— Tarred Road

- - - Unpaved road

· · · · · Footpath

■ Building

+ Church

▲ Triangulation pillar or other landmark

🍺 Pub

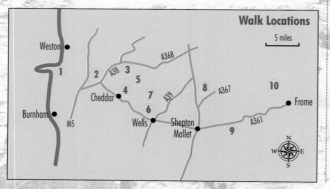

Walk Locations

5 miles

Weston

Burnham

Cheddar

Wells

Shepton Mallet

Frome

1 2 3 5 4 7 6 8 9 10

A368 A38 A39 A367 A361 M5

N
W E
S

1 Brean Down & Bristol Channel

Coastal extremity of the Mendip Hills

This, together with offshore Steep Holm, is the western extremity of the Mendip Hills. Jutting out into the turbid waters of the Bristol Channel, Brean Down promontory is a virtual island, and a literal one when the Somerset Levels suffer one of their periodic inundations. The 160-acre headland, owned by the National Trust, rises a theoretical 320 feet above the adjoining shipping lane. That height is variable as the Bristol Channel rises and falls up to 42 feet every 13

Level: 🐾 🐾
Length: 4 miles
Terrain: One stiff but short climb and a couple of lesser slopes.
Park & start: The car-park at **Brean Down Cafe** is beside the northern extremity of the coast road from Brean, Berrow and Burnham-on-Sea.
Start ref: ST 297 586 **Postcode:** TA8 2RS
Public transport: Buses from Burnham to Brean village.
Wesbistes: www.burnham-on-sea.com
www.nationaltrust.org.uk

hours, which is almost the largest tidal range on Earth (second only to the Bay of Fundy in Canada). That is why, if and when it is built, Brean Down will be on the front-line for a Severn Energy barrage.

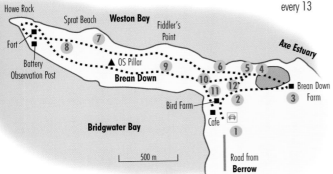

Howe Rock
Sprat Beach **Weston Bay** Fiddler's Point
Fort
8   7
Axe Estuary
Battery
Observation Post
▲ OS Pillar   9   6   5   4
Brean Down   10
11   12   ■ Brean Down
2   3   Farm
Bird Farm
Cafe 🚗
Bridgwater Bay
1
|— 500 m —|
Road from
Berrow

1 Set off along the access road (NE) on the inland side of the Cafe and Bird Farm to the foot of the escarpment in 250 metres.

2 Ignore the incline road and stay on the bottom one (E) to **Brean Down Farm** in 350 metres.

3 Here the track splits in three directions but we take none of them. Instead you turn sharply left (NW) beside telegraph pole No. 9 which is 25 metres from the garages. Beside it a narrow public path rises uphill through a carpet of ivy and cuckoo pint.

Sand castle in the Cove

Brean Down Harbour was to have been the national terminal for mail packets to the West Indies, with the foundation stone laid by Lady Eardley Wilmot on 5 November 1864, but it was wrecked by a storm on 9 December 1872.

4 In 100 metres we cross the fence-line into the promontory above the farm. Glance back down on the **River Axe** snaking into its estuary. Proceed via another couple of stiles to join the top of the incline road on the summit in a further 200 metres.

Beach Café

6 Now follow the main track which becomes a coast path (NW) above **Fiddler's Point** in 500 metres. In another 500 metres (W) we pass above the extremity of Weston-super-Mare's mud, off **Sprat Beach**, which used to sustain a considerable fishery.

Palmerstonian fortifications

5 Turn right here (E), along the top of the outcrops, for a better view over Uphill and the mud-flats around Black Rock from somewhere towards the end of the headland in 350 metres. This diversion is your best chance of seeing flocks of duck, geese and waders. Then re-trace your steps (W) to the top of the incline.

7 In a further 500 metres you approach the Palmerstonian **Brean Down Fort** which shared its role of an anti-ship gun battery across the Bristol Channel with Steep Holm, an island, three miles offshore. Royal Engineers and the Royal Artillery re-established it for the Fixed Defences Severn in July 1941. Explore the relics of both periods, spread over the

next 150 metres, plus an experimental rocket launcher set into the tip of the headland beside **Howe Rock**.

8 On returning inland from the bridge over the dry-moat at the fort we bear right (ESE). Pass between the concrete emplacements for two Second World War 6-inch

Rocket rails and searchlight post

guns and then pass the **Battery Observation Post**. Ensure you keep to the **Weston Bay** side of the rim of the cliffs - that's our side of the slope - as you approach the Ordnance Survey triangulation pillar in 500 metres.

9 Proceed across the humps and hollows of an Iron Age settlement into a dip in another 500 metres. From here we climb (E) to the traces of a platform in 100 metres which marks the site of a Roman temple.

10 In the next stage of 500 metres we pass a Bronze Age round barrow. Again follow a well-trodden path on the Weston side of the outcrops and keep them to your right. A precipice falls away to **Bridgwater Bay** on the other side.

Weston Bay

11 Our car-park is now visible. You have two options. Either turn right (S) down the flight of steps, the direct route back of 300 metres, or proceed along the summit.

12 The second option brings us back via the access road (E), in 400 metres, and then a further 400 metres to return via the incline (SW) and the road from the farm.

2 **Wavering Down & Crook Peak**

National Trust access land rings the wild hills on this 6-mile route

Something of the expanse and scale of the mediaeval royal Mendip Forest hunting ground survives across the unenclosed landscape of King's Wood and Wavering Down. The woodland is ancient - either of Anglo-Saxon or Norman date - and includes pollarded specimens of the rare small-leaved lime. Limestone grassland across the slopes above gives way to windswept outcrops which rise into a Dartmoor-like Tor on Crook Peak. This may have been named for someone called Crook but locals insist it took its name from its shepherd's crook outline

Level: 🥾 🥾
Length: 6 miles
Terrain: Open access common land and woods with rocky outcrops.
Park & start: From the National Trust carpark on **Winscombe Hill** which is reached along an inconspicuous turning westwards off the A38 between the northern Axbridge turn-off and the **Texaco** filling station on top of the hill.
Start ref: ST 422 560 **Postcode:** BS25 1DH
Public transport: Buses between Axbridge and Winscombe.
Websites: www.comptonbishopfamilies.co.uk
www.frankiehowerd.com

which has become a familiar silhouette for drivers on the M5. These days horned White Park cattle do the conservation grazing.

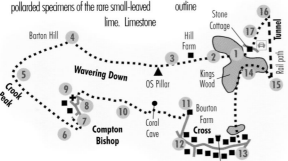

Barton Hill — 4
5
Crook Peak
9
8
7
6
Compton Bishop
Coral Cave
OS Pillar
Wavering Down
10
Kings Wood
11 Bourton Farm
Cross
12
13
White Hart Inn
3
2
1
Hill Farm
Stone Cottage
16
17
Tunnel
Rail path
14
15

500 m

① Set off through the gate, to the left of **Stone Cottage**, into **King's Wood**. Spot the limekiln attached to the end of the cottage. Continue straight ahead (W), uphill along a stony bridleway which is an ancient road flanked on the right by an Anglo-Saxon boundary bank.

The peak from the down

Stone Cottage and limekiln

② In 400 metres you can glimpse **The Hall,** in trees to the right, and the path brings us into a dip to the left of **Hill Farm** in another 900 metres. **Wavering Down** extends to our left.

③ Continue to follow the wall up the slope to the Ordnance Survey triangulation pillar, on a denuded cairn at 690 feet above sea level, in 500 metres. Carry on following the wall for 800 metres, and as it bears right (NW) for 300 metres.

④ We now bear left (SW) on **Barton Hill** to head directly towards the snout-like profile of **Crook Peak**. The rocky crags rise in 1,000 metres into an outcrop 627 feet above the sea-level M5 motorway. The seaward view is across the Bristol

Channel to the Millennium Stadium in Cardiff.

5 Turn left (SE) to head inland towards Glastonbury Tor, the glasshouses of Tanyard Farm Nurseries, and humped Nyland Hill rising from the Somerset Levels. We descend gradually along the crest-line of the exposed strata into grassland beyond. In 900 metres we look down to the left on the church tower at Compton Bishop.

Crook Peak is the barren focal-point of 726 acres of common land, including King's Wood, which was bought by the National Trust in 1986.

6 Proceed for a further 300 metres to fence bars near the bottom of the main grassy slope. Turn left in 10 metres (NW), into a rocky path through the trees, to descend to a stone wall in 100 metres. Keep this to your right and continue straight ahead to a gate in 75 metres.

7 Here we bear right (NE) in a deep-cut trackway to leave National Trust land and pass **Glebe House** in 50 metres. **Vicarage Lane** brings us into **Compton Bishop** in 150 metres.

8 Turn left (NW) up **Butts Batch** - beside **Manor Farm** - to **St Andrew's Church** in 150 metres.

Crook Peak summit

9 Turn right, down **Church Lane** (N), to the junction in 100 metres at the bottom of the hill. Proceed straight ahead, into the drive beside **Longbourne**, which is a public path. This bends to the right (E) to skirt gardens and follow electricity poles around to a stile in the corner of the stable yard beside **Glastonbury Thorn** in 150 metres.

10 Continue straight ahead (E), across four fields, over stiles, and keep the hedgerow to your right. In 800 metres we go through a gate and follow the fence, with the rocky escarpment of **Wavering Down** and **Coral Cave** to the left. Pass to the left of a house and its lawn. Cross more stiles.

From the reign of Edward VI, the Prowse family held Compton Bishop for generations, with Thomas Prowse - the last of the line - erecting a great white marble monument in the nave of St Andrew's Church, in 1751.

11 In 400 metres we come to **Bourton Farm**. Join **Bourton Lane** and turn right (S) along it to **Webbington Lane** in 400 metres.

12 Turn left (E), passing the home of actor Frankie Howerd, and continue straight ahead at the junction with the **Old Coach Road** in 300 metres. Proceed through **Cross** hamlet to the **White Hart Inn** in 500 metres.

13 In a further 200 metres, after **Moorland House** and **Justaway Cottages** but before the 'give way' sign, we turn left (N) up into a narrow and rocky bridleway for 150 metres. This brings us back into National Trust land where we bear

Green woodpeckers (listen for their 'yaffle' cries) and buzzards (much given to mewing) breed in and around King's Wood.

right across the foothills of **Wavering Down**. Continue straight ahead along the bridleway to a gate into **King's Wood** in 750 metres.

14 Keep taking right-hand options but stay inside the boundary fence to the next gate in 750 metres. Follow the fence (NE) to a stile in the corner in 50 metres. Turn right (SE) and join the disused **Cheddar Valley Railway** in 200 metres.

15 Turn left (N) to the tunnel entrance in 150 metres. Continue straight through it to light on the other side in 200 metres.

16 Go on for about 250 metres on the other side. Then turn left (W), up a flight of 12 steps, to a kissing gate into a field. Turn left

The en route subterranean treat is along the course of Cheddar Valley Railway - known as the Strawberry Line - which was cut through Winscombe Hill in 1869 and closed in 1964.

Light beyond the tunnel

(SW) and walk up the grassy slope between the wooded railway bank and the other band of trees in 300 metres.

17 Go through the kissing gate at the top end of the field and drop down into a deep-cut track. Turn left, up through the gully, to return in 100 metres to the road and car-park at **Stone Cottage**.

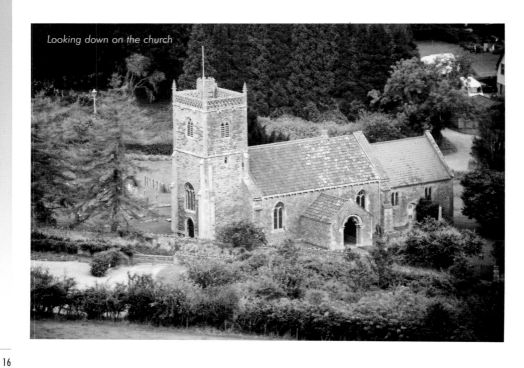

Looking down on the church

3 Burrington & Dolebury

*Common land with classic caves and
an iconic cleft in the cliffs*

A long from the famous Rock of Ages,
our second offering is Aveline's Hole,
which has been rising in status since the
advent of scientific archaeology.
Reappraisal of its bones and the careful
way they were laid out has confirmed
that it contained the earliest known
cemetery in prehistoric Europe.

Numerous other caves and holes pepper
the sides and toplands of Burrington
Combe. Many contained evidence of
woolly rhinoceros and hyena, and their
meals, and doubled as shelters for
Palaeolithic man in the tundra on the
edge of receding arctic ice towards the
end of Earth's last great global cooling.

Level: 🐾 🐾 🐾
Length: 5 miles
Terrain: Wild landscape with challenging
vegetation crossed by a network of rocky paths.
Park and start: In **Burrington
Combe**, in the layby with the public toilets
beside the B3134, beside the cattle-grid
100 metres south of **Burrington Inn**.
Start ref: ST 477 587 **Postcode:** BS18 7AT
Public transport: Bus stop at the start
point, for the Chew Valley Explorer.
Websites: www.burringtoninn.co.uk
www.tripadvisor.co.uk

Where there is something visible beside
or near our route, it will be pointed out,
but these one-time refuges come with a
modern health warning. Look at them
from the outside, in daylight, but do not
venture into the darkness.

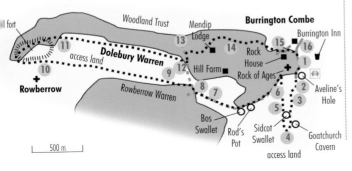

1 Set off into the Combe (S) and cross the road in 50 metres see the **Rock of Ages**. In another 65 metres, just around the sharp bend, go back to the other side to gaze into the cavernous mouth of **Aveline's Hole** which descends from just beside the road at an angle of 30 degrees.

2 Follow the B3134 for another 200 metres, around the next corner and along a straight section of road, to a rough track which forks off to the right (SW) about 50 metres before the brow of the hill. This path becomes the bed of a disappearing stream - lots in Mendip do this - and in 50 metres you see the reason. Up to the right, 10 metres away, is **Sidcot Swallet**. This narrow hole

beneath a yew tree is named for the Quaker boys of Sidcot School who were first to explore it.

3 Continue upstream for 35 metres to a spot 10 metres down from a concrete trough from which clear water flows. Turn sharp left and then right to walk up the path for 80 metres. Pass a small hole form which a cool draught blows, to notorious **Goatchurch Cavern**, where Mendip Cave Rescue service has seen most of its emergencies.

4 Return to the trough and carry on up the slope for 25 metres. We emerge from hawthorn scrub into a bracken-covered hillside. Continue uphill to a cross-roads of paths in 75 metres.

Rock of Ages

5 Here we turn right (N) with the gorge-like slopes of Burrington Combe now being glimpsed to our right. Stay on the main track as it swings to the left in 50 metres. Then in another 40 metres it bends to the right as another minor track joins from the left. In

120 metres we cross a wide track and take the right-hand of the two paths facing us on the other side. Continue to the edge of **Mendip Lodge Wood** in 250 metres. If you get lost, just make for this wooded skyline.

6 Turn left (SW), along the well marked track, with trees to your right and bracken to the left. In 500 metres - which is difficult to gauge - in one a hollow down to the left a couple of holes drop into **Rod's Pot**. Next on the left, in 75 metres, is **Bos Swallet**.

7 In 300 metres our onward track (W) approaches the conifer woods of **Rowberrow Warren**. In a gully to the left, a stream disappears into hole in the rock-face, and 10 metres upwards and to the right is a slit in the ground that descends into **Read's Cavern**. The main track continues downhill (NW) to a cross-roads of stony tracks in 300 metres.

8 Turn right here (N), up the track, for 100 metres.

9 Turn left (W) to enter National Trust land at **Dolebury Warren**. Take the grassy track, straight ahead, to a gate in 300 metres. Again continue straight ahead, along the path that follows the whole length of the southern slope. In a further 1,250 metres we reach a stony bank at the lower corner of **Dolebury** hill-fort.

(10) Follow the outer earthwork and pass the tower of **Rowberrow Church** which is down

The hymn 'Rock of Ages' by Augustus Montague Toplady, inspired by the cleft in the rocks at Burrington Combe where the curate from Blagdon sheltered from a storm, first appeared in print in the Gospel Magazine in 1775.

Study group storming Dolebury

to the left. In 500 metres we bear right and enter the hill-fort, to cross it diagonally (NE) and climb the rocky slope to the top corner in another 500 metres. Here we have the finest view in Mendip, of Crook Peak, Brean Down, and Steep Holm and the wider landscape to Wales and Bristol.

(11) Continue straight ahead (E), with woodland to your left, and go through the gate to pass through a conifer clump in 500 metres. Again continue ahead, into open grassland with **Dolebury Warren Wood** to your left and our earlier path across to the right.

Dolebury Warren, 225 acres of barren heather moorland, has a viewpoint Iron Age hill-fort with its inner rampart standing 20 feet high, contrasting with low pillow-like mounds constructed by mediaeval rabbit keepers.

(12) Go through the gate in the stone wall ahead of you, near the corner of the pasture, under the line of beech trees. Turn left along the stony track (N) for 100 metres to a Woodland Trust gate to your left, and continue along the main track for a further 120 metres, to the second Woodland Trust gate.

(13) Turn right (E), opposite this gate, for 30 metres and then turn left at the next path junction, to follow the track (NE) down to the romantic ruin of **Mendip Lodge** which we pass in 150 metres. Keep its outer wall and arches to your right.

Hill-fort rampart

(14) Follow the main track through the laurels of **Mendip Lodge Wood** which belongs to Langford Court Estate. Continue straight ahead along this public footpath which gradually descends to a road at **Link** in 1,200 metres.

15 Turn left, downhill, for 100 metres. Turn right, immediately after the garden of **Rock House**, down a narrow path across rocks to **Link Cottage** in 150 metres.

16 Turn right (S), along its drive, which was the main road for Edwardian charabancs entering **Burrington Combe**. This joins the replacement modern road which passes the **Burrington Inn** and brings us back to the cattle-grid and car-park in 300 metres.

Mendip Lodge

4 Cheddar Gorge & Black Rock

World-famous offerings in the most rewarding of 4-mile circuits

This is spectacular landform geology. The rocky canyon, of grey limestone cliffs rising precipitously to tower 450 feet above the valley floor, seems to have lost its water. That is only because it has gone underground and is scouring out fresh caverns in the process. A total of 429 acres of the tumbling western slopes and cliffs, including the Lion Rock and Black Rock, were acquired by the National Trust between 1910 and 1998. The opposite heights of Cheddar Cliffs and the Pinnacles were sold by Sir Edward Seymour to Sir John Thynne

Level: 🥾 🥾 🥾
Length: 4 miles
Terrain: A 'strenuous scramble' according to English Nature, with rough going across exposed rocks.
Park and start: In Cheddar, either in a car-park or on a back street beyond the parking restrictions, and begin the walk from Cliff Street.
Start ref: ST 462 537 **Postcode:** BS27 3PX
Public transport: Buses from Axbridge to Wells.
Websites: www.cheddarcaves.co.uk
www.mendiphillsaonb.org.uk

in Elizabethan times and descended to the Marquess of Bath. These and the cave systems beneath remain outlying possessions of the Longleat Estate.

Piney Sleight
Nature Reserve
6
7
5
8
Cheddar Cliffs
9
Black Rock
Tuttors Hill
3
4
10 The Pinnacles
Water Lane
Wind Rock
2
Caves
High Rock
Birch Hill
13
11
500 m
1
14
Jacob's Ladder
12
Lookout Tower
Cheddar Riverside Inn

Cheddar Cliffs

① Set off from the **Riverside Inn** (N), opposite **Frog Cottage** and beside **Cheddar Fish Bar**, up **Birch Hill**. In 250 metres we turn left (NW), along **Water Lane**, and rise to the junction with **Silver Street** in 50 metres.

② Turn right (NE), up **Tuttors Hill**, for 250 metres. Turn right after the second corner, between **Vine Cottage** and **Rockwell House**. ARC's workings in Batt's Combe dent the western skyline, with distant Axbridge and Crook Peak rising beyond Cheddar Reservoir.

③ Our route is the other way (SE) beside **Apple Tree Cottage** to **Cufic House**. In 150 metres we bear left (E), up a sloping terrace, into scrubby woodland. The rocky path climbs to a gate in the right-hand stone wall, between yew trees, in 350 metres.

④ Turn left (NE) through thickets of hazel and blackthorn. In 250 metres we cross a stile. Here we turn right (S), following the stone wall, which then bends (E) around the top of the central section of **Cheddar Gorge**. We are now on National Trust land. There are coppiced hazel stands across the wall to the right and a dramatic glimpse of the eastern Gorge.

⑤ In 500 metres, at the corner of this wild area of limestone grassland, we continue straight ahead (NE) across a stile. Follow the rocky

Black Rock

slope at the top of the Gorge with a fence to your left.

6 After a gate and stile in 600 metres the path goes up and over **Piney Sleight** into the upper end of the Gorge. Here we descend, still following the fence to our left, down into a valley in 300 metres.

7 Continue straight ahead, across the stone stile, at the foot of the grassy slope. The path

(SE) then enters hazel woodland and brings us to the main track through a nature reserve, at **Black Rock**, in 350 metres.

8 Turn right (W) to **Cliff Road** - through the Gorge - in 100 metres. Cross to the stile beside the bus-stop and climb uphill through the wood. This is another stiff and boulder-strewn climb (SW). At the top, in 350 metres, we emerge from the trees and go through a gate into hawthorn scrubland.

> *'Cheder Hole' - to use the original spelling - was chosen by 12th-century chronicler Henry of Huntingdon as one of his four wonders of England.*

Rocky path

9 Proceed straight ahead (W) to a path junction in 50 metres. Here bear right, along the grassy option, into an area of bracken and boulders.

10 Cross the stile in 400 metres and then turn left (SW). Hereon you must keep this fence to your left, and in sight where possible, and avoid being enticed by alternative paths off to the right. These end in free-fall at the Pinnacles, Wind Rock and High Rock. From there the cars down in the Gorge look like Dinky toys. Leave the precipice to the climbers and the Cheddar pink which is its niche rock-plant.

11 Our path meanders in a gradual descent to the cliffs above **Gough's Cave** in 800 metres. Ahead is Cheddar village with Nyland Hill and Cheddar Reservoir beyond in the Levels.

12 In 300 metres we pass **Pulpit Rock** - smothered in undergrowth to the right - and proceed to the top of **Jacob's Ladder**, 50 metres before reaching the **Lookout Tower** built by Rowland Pavey in 1920. Both are now part of Cheddar Showcaves.

13 Descend Jacob's Ladder to the cafe, turnstile and shop in 150 metres. Here you have the opportunity to visit **Cox's Cave**.

14 Turn left (W), beside the ponds, to return to **Cliff Street** in 300 metres.

Carboniferous limestone of the Mendip Hills was laid down in the warm seas of 330 million years ago and subsequently uplifted by collision of tectonic plates as Africa drifted into Europe.

5 Charterhouse & Lead Mines

An industrial zone from the Romans to the Victorians reverts to nature

Boulders and slag-heaps of galena (its Latin name) litter the Charterhouse landscape. This de-leaded ore looks like lumps of black glass peppered with minute air pockets. Rakes on the hilltop above Bleak House are believed to be of Roman date. Tiberius Claudius Trifolius, running these mines in Vespasian's time, seems to have been too successful. Pliny, in his Historia Naturalis, records that before AD 77 a law was enacted to restrict the production of British lead to relieve competition on the Spanish mines. Lead was used for plumbing (another Latin word), caskets, coffins and weights. Added value came from the fact that Mendip lead has a 0.04 per cent silver content.

Level: 🥾 🥾
Length: 5 miles
Terrain: One steep slope but otherwise ordinary decent paths.
Park and start: In **Charterhouse-on-Mendip** nature reserve car-park at the end of the 300 metres cul-de-sac lane beside **Charterhouse Outdoor Education** Centre which is reached from the B3134 between the Castle of Comfort Inn and the top of Burrington Combe.
Start ref: ST 505 557 **Postcode:** BS40 7XR
Public transport: None
Websites: www.romanbritain.org.uk/places
www.swgfl.org.uk/charterhouse

Map labels

8
7
Masts
9
Roman Amphitheatre
Rains Batch
Water Works
6
Fernbrook
Townfield
10
Blackmoor
Nether Wood
11 12
Lead Works
Charterhouse
✝
13
nature reserve
1
2
5
Mendips Adventure Base
Long Wood
4
Velvet Bottom
Black Rock nature reserve
3

500 m

27

1 Set off down into the valley, through the gate beside the entrance to the car-park, on the left-hand side of the road (SW). There is a Roman quarry shaft up on the slope to your right and the 'buddles' and settling pools below date from the Victorian final phase of the lead workings.

Starting point

2 Turn right (W) on reaching the road in 300 metres and then left (SW), in 60 metres, to re-enter the nature reserve. Pass the Mendip Adventure Base in 500 metres.

Mineral resources were a key reason for the Roman invasion of Britain and within six years of the conquest the mines at Charterhouse were producing lead and silver.

Continue straight ahead along the entirety of **Velvet Bottom**, passing numerous signs of industrial archaeology, for 1,500 metres.

3 We arrive at a five-way path junction at a corkscrew turn in the valley system. Here we turn right (NW) on joining the first path and then right again (NE) in 75 metres.

4 Climb the steep hillside, diagonally, with the next Somerset Wildlife Trust reserve being directly behind you, on National Trust land at **Black Rock**. In 300 metres we reach the right-hand corner of **Long Wood** and continue straight ahead (N), keeping the trees to our left, for another 300 metres.

Four pigs of lead (weight 562 pounds) constituted a Roman cart-load and were stamped 'BRIT EX ARG' - from the British lead and silver mines - which were run by a procurator as a nationalised industry.

5 In the next field we bear right (NE), diagonally, to the far corner in 500 metres. Also bear right in the next field, down to the bottom right-hand corner, in 300 metres. Continue through the wood (N) to the stream and road beside the first bungalow at **Fernbrook** in 100 metres.

6 Cross the road and stile to keep the stream and under-growth in the gully to your left (NNE).

Ignore a path that branches off to the left into the **Bristol Waterworks** woods in 300 metres.

7 Our path (N) continues up the right-hand side of the valley to cross-roads of tracks in the dip on the summit in 800 metres.

'Gruffy ground' at Charterhouse - hummocks, hollows and holes - dates from the Middle Ages through to peak demand during the Civil War.

Lead mines

(8) Turn right (E) along this double-hedged trackway, which turns from green grass to grey ballast, to the communications masts - at 1,020 feet above sea level - in 900 metres.

(9) Turn right (SE) down stony **Rains Batch**. The amphitheatre of Roman Charterhouse, with an oval bank 15 feet above its arena, can be glimpsed in the first field on the right in 250 metres. In another 400 metres we pass **Townfield**

bungalow. The field beside and behind it covers the remains of a small Roman mining town. In 150 metres we reach the tarred road.

(10) Turn right (SW) to a roadside stile in 200 metres.

(11) Turn left here (SE), down to the stream and ponds, in **Blackmoor** in 200 metres, where we enter the nature reserve. Proceed straight ahead to the main valley path in 150 metres.

Recycling of much of the old slag took place between 1844 and 1855, as residual lead was removed by improved refining methods, but the industry then collapsed as cheap materials were imported from the British Empire.

Industrial pool

(12) Turn right for our onward path (S) but pause first for optional diversions. Turn left for 100 metres and then right for 150 metres, up the slope beside **Nether Wood** to the trees at Nordrach, to see lines of condenser-tubes from Victorian furnaces. On returning to the main path and turning left, look across the valley floor to the platform on the other side, which is formed by the earthworks of a playing-card shaped Roman fort.

Roman mine

Lead slag

(13) Fork right in 300 metres, on joining the stony byway from Nordrach, and again skirt 'buddles' and settling pools to return to the car-park in another 150 metres.

Condensing tubes

6 Ebbor & Wookey

Five miles of rocky and undergound Mendip, from an extinct river-bed through to the real-life River Axe, gushing out of the cave that has given the village its name

Ebbor Gorge is a miniature Cheddar Gorge - without the cars. Caves and rock-shelters have yielded artefacts from the Upper Palaeolithic to Romano-British period. They are now kept from human intrusion for the benefit of the lesser horseshoe bat. Wild woods, covering 142 acres, are a National Nature Reserve. The core area was given to the National Trust by Mrs Julia Cazalet Hodgkinson in 1967 in memory of Sir Winston Churchill. The famous Wookey Hole Caves, with spectacular stalagmites and stalactites

Level: 🐾 🐾 🐾
Length: 5 miles
Terrain: Rocky, rough and rugged in places.
Park and start: Half a mile above Ebbor Farm, Wookey Hole, in the **National Nature Reserve** car-park for Ebbor Gorge which is concealed in **Ebbor Woods**.
Start ref: ST 521 485 **Postcode:** BA5 1AY
Public transport: Buses from Wells to Wookey Hole where you join the walk en route.
Websites:
www.englishnature.org.uk/specialsites
www.wookey.co.uk

as well as a subterranean stretch of the River Axe, can also be included in the menu - if you buy a ticket.

national nature reserve

Deerleap

Ebbor Gorge

Ebbor Woods

Mendip Hills

Wookey Hole entrance

Paper Mill

Myrtle Farm

Green Lane

Wookey House

Wookey Hole Inn

Milton Lane

Tynings Lane

Pear Tree Cottage

Wookey Hole

500 m

1 Set off from the top end of the car-park. Turn right, across the stone stile, and descend the flight of steps (SE).

2 In 400 metres the path continues straight ahead, uphill. Turn sharp left here (N). Head downhill towards the Gorge.

3 Cross the footbridge in 80 metres. Follow the stream (SE) for 200 metres. At this junction of paths we turn left (N). Begin to climb up the course of a prehistoric river-bed. In 350 metres, towering crags emerge from the trees, and the track coils into a rocky ascent. The slopes are initially draped in ivy, ferns and mosses and then you pass an active scree slope to enter the upstanding geology.

4 Continue upwards along the path through the middle of **Ebbor Gorge**. From the cleft in the rocks in 200 metres you have a view across the northern Levels to the Polden Hills. This must have been a spectacular waterfall, either flowing or frozen, at the end of the Ice Age.

5 In 150 metres we come to a path junction. Turn right (S), uphill, for 50 metres to the top of the slope. Now turn left (E) at the cross-roads of woodland paths, to continue our upward progress.

6 Exit from the wood at the stile and gate in 150 metres. Continue straight ahead, uphill across limestone grassland, and pass a drinking pool in 250 metres. Beyond

Entering Ebbor

Rising from the 1,001-feet contour on the Mendip Hills, the television transmission mast reaches an altitude of 1,995 feet - making it the highest point in Somerset.

it we leave the nature reserve by crossing the stile by the gate. Continue uphill towards the television mast. Look across the main part of the Somerset Levels to the entire line of the Quantock Hills and Exmoor beyond. Landmarks range from Alfred's Tower and Glastonbury Tor to Hinkley Point. This remarkable view is more than 70 miles wide.

 7 Keep following the fence, around to the left (SE), but

do not cross the stile between the two gates in 350 metres. Here we leave the Priddy path and continue to head for the mast. Drop down into the next corner of the field in 150 metres and cross the stile above the gate. Follow

the hedge and wall (E) for 600 metres.

8 Cross the stile beside the gate. Here we leave the path that heads for the mast and bear right

Hilltop watering hole

Paper Mills

to descend along a second path (SE) that drops towards Manor Farm and the city of Wells. In 250 metres we cross a stile beside a gate and enter stony **Green Lane**.

(9) In 250 metres we go through a gate, and then another in 150 metres, and a third in 400 metres. The next gate is in 100 metres. From here we follow the hedge (S) down to a road in 150 metres.

(10) Turn right (W) along **Tynings Lane**. Continue straight ahead at the junction in 100 metres. Then pass **Pear Tree Cottage** on the corner and bear left beside it (SW) into **Myrtle Lane** in 30 metres.

(11) Pass 1689-dated **Myrtle Farm** and follow the road down to the junction in **Wookey Hole** village in 600 metres.

(12) Turn right (N) to pass the former **Wesleyan Chapel**, **Homestead Stores**, **Wookey Hole Club**, **Wookey Hole Inn** and **St Mary Magdalen Church**.

The Axe above ground

Bear left (NW) in 350 metres, on approaching the Mill on the corner.

13 Cross the bridge and then turn right (N) in 100 metres between **Bubwith Corner Cottage** and the sign 'This road is not suitable for charabancs'. The ravine leads to the hole from which the **River Axe** gushes into daylight from its subterranean passage through the Mendip Hills.

14 Halfway along this tarred path, in 175 metres, we turn left (NW), along an unsurfaced public path into the trees beside a hazel bush. This dirt track takes us up through the wooded slope to a stile in 150 metres. Cross the pasture (W) to the gates in 100 metres.

15 Do not go through any gate but instead turn left (S) along the track down to the farm buildings. We are now heading towards Glastonbury Tor. Descend to the road between **Wookey** **House** and **Ebbor House** in 250 metres.

16 Turn right (NW), uphill, passing former mill-workers' cottages. In 125 metres we turn right (NE), beside the bungalow, into a stony green lane signed to Priddy. Bear left (N) in 50 metres and follow the hedge into a dry valley with an extensive badger sett up in the terrace to the right.

17 In 350 metres we cross a stile beside the gate into to **Ebbor Gorge National Nature Reserve**. Proceed for 300 metres (NW) to the path junction and then follow signs to the left, up the steep slope, to return to the car-park in 500 metres.

Describing Wookey Hole, Titus Flavius Clemens of Alexandria gave Somerset its first mention in world literature in 200AD.

The Axe underground

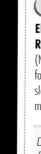

7 Priddy & Nine Barrows

Heart of Mendip in a 6-mile circuit with two taverns,
the sheep fair, skyline barrows and the last lead-works

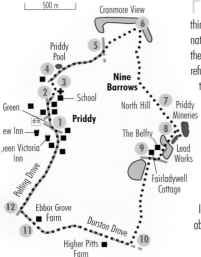

Level: 🥾 🥾
Length: 6 miles
Terrain: Boggy through the Mineries but otherwise gentle going across Mendip's rolling toplands.
Park and start: Beside the green in Priddy village which is reached from the A39 or the B3135.
Start ref: ST 527 509 **Postcode:** BA5 3BB
Public transport: None.
Websites: priddy.somerset.org.uk
    somerset.gov.uk/her/details

Priddy lies in the middle of Mendip's central plateau. It is still a centre for things agricultural, climbing, mining and natural history. Into the 20th century, the Extended Mining Company smelted refuse from the ancient ore washings that had brought so much wealth to the Bishops of Bath and Wells. Spreading across 123 acres, Priddy Mineries is now the principal local site of special scientific interest, being one of Mendip's best reptile and amphibian hot-spots. Lizards and snakes sun themselves on black lead-slag and there are toads in abundance around the lake and ponds.

Archaeology remains noticeable, with lines of Bronze Age burial mounds, studding the skyline. Priddy Fair - a traditional West Country sheep fair - is held annually on the Wednesday closest to 21 August.

(1) Set off across the village green (N) from the **New Inn** and continue along the lane beside the farm to the next area of open space on the hillside in 400 metres.

(2) Turn right (NE). Head for **St Laurence's Church** in 200 metres. Bear left beside the tower (NW) to follow the churchyard hedge, with a Bronze Age burial mound in the field on the other side, to your right.

The public fountain on Priddy Green carries a plaque for its provider: 'Pure water was brought here by James Green Esq., Lord of the Manor, October 1865.'

(3) Proceed to the sycamore tree and the next cluster of cottages in 250 metres.

(4) Turn right along **Nine Barrow Lane** (NE) and pass **Priddy Pool** beside the green lane in 250 metres. In a further 800 metres we come out of the trees into a wide corner with East Water Drove emerging from undergrowth to the right. There is a kissing gate into the field beside it.

(5) Enter this field and cross it diagonally to the gate between the conifers of roadside **Cranmore View** in the far corner. Here, in 650 metres, we turn sharp right (S) but stay inside the same pasture. With the trees now across to

James Green's well

the left we climb to **Priddy Nine Barrows** (actually eight in number) in 300 metres and pass between the skyline burial mounds.

(6) Continue to the two barrows, on the spur near the corner of the field, in 400 metres. Keep them

Stonecrop

to your right and cross the stile in the fence in 50 metres. Then follow the right-hand wall (SE) with seven more burial mounds on the other side, across **North Hill**, and enter the wild land of **Priddy Mineries** in 600 metres.

7 Follow the wall down to **Fair Lady Well** and the pools and tramways of former **St Cuthbert's Lead Works** in 500 metres.

8 Turn right (SW), avoiding the main track beside the pond, to pass between **St Cuthbert's Swallet** to the left and **The Belfry** immediately to your right in 400 metres. In a further 100 metres we emerge on the road beside **Rose Cottage**.

Largest of the Bronze Age burial mounds at Priddy Nine Barrows, the southernmost is 150 feet in diameter and 10 feet high - with a spot height upon it for 1,000 feet above sea level - making this the highest point hereabouts.

9 Turn right (W). Then turn left (S) at the stile, in 200 metres, just after **Fairladywell Cottage**. Keep the trees to your right as you follow the Monarch's Way. In 1,300 metres, the stone wall brings us to gates and a crossing of tracks, close to a power line.

10 Turn right here (NW), along **Durston Drove**, and keep

Nine Barrows

Higher Pitts Farm to your left in 300 metres. In 600 metres we ignore a footpath off to the right and continue along the droveway

which bears left (WSW). It brings us to **Ebbor Grove Farm** in a further 600 metres.

(11) Here the drove becomes the farm drive (NW) to the road at **Moor View** in 250 metres.

(12) Turn right (NE) to return along **Pelting Drove** - which becomes **Pelting Road** - to the **Queen Victoria Inn** in 1,200 metres and the **New Inn** around the corner in a further 200 metres.

Manor Farm and the section of royal Mendip Forest hunting ground around Priddy, which was granted to St Swithun's Priory at Winchester, with the saint's name becoming corrupted to 'Swildon' in Somerset speech.

Sheep Fair

Fair crowd at the Queen Victoria Inn

Stacked sheep hurdles

Priddy Green

The Mineries

8 Oakhill & Maesbury

Village brewery, Woodland Trust wood and a prehistoric hill-fort

Level: 💜💜
Length: 6 miles
Terrain: Relatively gentle though with a couple of moderate climbs.
Park and start: At **Oakhill**, in the High Street in the vicinity of Oakhill Brewery and the Post Office.
Start ref: ST 634 473 **Postcode:** BA3 5AS
Public transport: Buses between Shepton Mallet and Bath.

The Fosse Way, which we follow over the Mendip Hills, was the first frontier road of the Roman province of Britannia, cutting across country from Exeter to Lincoln. The walk peaks at Maesbury Castle, dating from 3rd century BC, which is a stoutly-defended Iron Age hill-fort. A single deep ditch and a massive bank protected a 7-acre domed plateau. There used to be visible hut-circles. Down in the village, the main trading name for the past couple of centuries has been the Oakhill Brewery. It was founded in 1767 by entrepreneurs Jordan and Billingsley, who built themselves big houses in sylvan settings.

Map labels:

18 · A37 · Pound Lane · Oakhill Manor · 22 · Bath Road · 21

Maesbury Castle · 19 · 20 · High Street · Golf Links Lane · 1 · 2 · 3 · Zion Hill · 4

17 · 16 · Castlehill Wood · **Oakhill** · 5 · Tanyard Farm

…emarsh …arm · 15 · 14 · Fosse Way · 6

13 · Burnt House Farm · 12 · Mill House Farm · Millbrook Water Works · Woodland Trust

11 · 10 · A37 · 9 · 8 · Yollingmill Road · 7 · Beacon Farm

Windsor Hill Lane · Downside Inn

500 m

(1) Set off towards the main road (E) to the junction beside **The Tallet** in 50 metres. Turn left here (N) and climb **Zion Hill**. Turn right beside Dean Cottage, quirkily picturesque to fit the oddly shaped corner of Dean Lane, up the steep slope to Zion Cottage, Oakhill Manor and **Grange House** in 200 metres.

(2) Turn right here (E) into the sports field behind the village hall. Follow its southern boundary which you keep to your right. Go through the kissing gate in the corner in 250 metres and turn right (SE) to follow the fence down to the road. We reach it in 150 metres, left of **Oakhill Lodge** and the 1825-dated Wesleyan Chapel.

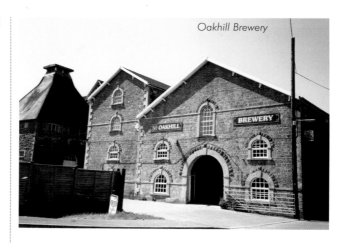

Oakhill Brewery

(3) Cross the main road to the kissing gate opposite and then bear right, to the stile to the left of school playground. Bear left in the next field, through parkland pasture, keeping the houses to your right. In 400 metres we come to a road opposite **Tresco** bungalow.

(4) Turn left along Fosse Way (E) to **Fosse Cottage** in 200 metres.

Zion Hill

(5) Turn right (SSW) just before **Fosse Farm** and **Tanyard Farm**. This double-hedged track is the **Fosse Way** which we follow upwards towards Ilchester - the next Roman town - with our back to Bath. In 400 metres there is a kink, westwards, from the original line for 250 metres. On resuming the real course we continue for another 600 metres.

Oakhill Brewery, which had its own 3-mile siding to the Somerset & Dorset Railway at Binegar Station, was 'renowned for its famous invalid stout', production of which reached 2,500 barrels a week.

(6) Cross the **Old Frome Road** (also Roman, Charterhouse lead mines) into **Beacon Wood** on the other side. This is a Woodland Trust property. There are Bronze Age burial mounds further along Beacon Hill. In 200 metres the Fosse Way resumes as a scrubby green lane. In 300 metres we come to a tarred road.

(7) Turn right (W) along **Yellingmill Lane** to **New Row** and **Millbrook Waterworks** in 600 metres. Just after the Bristol Water sign we turn left through the gate opposite the buildings.

(8) Two public paths cross this field. Ours bears right (SW)

The Fosse Way

up the slope. Exit from the far corner of the field, from the right-hand of triple kinks in the boundary. The hedgerow to our left now takes us towards the sound of main road traffic at **Upper Downside** in 200 metres.

(9) Cross the A37 beside **Mendip Lodge**, with a combination of caution and alacrity, to the stone stile on the other side. On this side of the road, down to your left, you have an opportunity for a midway diversion to the **Downside Inn**.

(10) On the path (W), across the hilltop pasture, we keep the northern hedge 150 metres to our right. In 500 metres we continue straight ahead, through the next hedge, and cross this field to a gate beside the lane in 100 metres, to the right of a road junction and house.

(11) Turn right along **Windsor Hill Lane** (N) for 100 metres. Turn left at the bend (NW),

The Beacon (976 feet above sea level) and Maesbury (974 feet) are the high points on the top of Mendip where it is crossed by the Fosse Way and its successor main road, the A37.

Beacon Wood

across stiles, beside a hunting gate. We cross a rushy meadow, once dammed, below **Mill House Farm**. In the following pasture we continue uphill and cross a stile beside the dense hedgerow which we keep to our right.

12 Cross the stile to the left of two gates and bear left across this much bigger field in 200 metres. Aim for a point to the left of Castle Hill Wood at the left-hand extremity of the visible section of the Mendip Hills. **Burnt House Farm** is further to our left and we follow the left-hand hedgerow towards it in another 200 metres. Cross a stile in the hedgerow in the corner of the field and proceed up the slope to the right of the barns (N).

Thrupemarsh Farm

13 Cross the drive into the right-hand field on the other side. Bear left across it (NW) towards Maesbury Castle. Bear right in the next field, to a gate in the opposite hedgerow, at the end of the cross-field line of oaks. Cross the stile to the left of the gate and join the western end of **Burnt House Drove** in 250 metres. Turn left along it, into the field beyond.

14 There are two public paths across this field. Our bears right, to the right of the Mendip television transmitter, as we head to the left of the farm - in 400 metres - and Castlehill Wood. Go through the gate into the field below **Thrupemarsh Farm** and cross it to the gate on the other side, between the barns and the farmhouse.

'Where mystery ends, religion begins,' wrote Dr James Foster who hid 'from the fury of bigots' in a summer house on Zion Hill until his death in 1753.

15 Walk up (N) to **Old Frome Road** in 200 metres. Turn left along it (NW), for 300 metres, to pass **Castlehill Wood**. Glastonbury Tor is clearly visible across to the left. Proceed for 200 metres beyond the wood.

16 Turn right across the stone stile beside the gate - into the field beyond the wood - just before the junction. Bear right (E), uphill, to the top end of the wood in

250 metres. Climb the stone stile and bear left (NE) up through the rampart of **Maesbury Castle**. Cross the centre of the Iron Age hill-fort and leave it via a stile beneath a beech tree in 200 metres. This is to the left of the western extremity of the adjoining golf course.

17 There is another stile beneath sycamores. Follow these trees and some sturdy beeches into the vale. Head towards the drone of the traffic, in an otherwise pastoral landscape, with **Furze Wood** across to the left and **Marsh Wood** over to the right.

18 Follow the hedgerow for 750 metres, almost to Roemead Road, but do not join it. Instead we

Maesbury

turn right (SE) and keep a dense hedgerow to the left with a field between it and the road. Cross a stream in the meadows. In 400 metres, after passing **Roemead Farm** - which is also a field away - we climb iron fence bars and our hedge then brings us to a stile in the next corner of the field.

(19) Enter a stub-end of leafy green lane which we follow (E) to a tarred road in 300 metres and then the A37, north of **Batts**

Farm, in a further 50 metres. Expect fast traffic on this stretch as you cross with utmost care towards Oakhill. Also continue straight ahead at the next cross-roads, with **Green Lane**, in 200 metres.

(20) Proceed for a further 175 metres and turn left (NNE) opposite the drive to the garage. Head to the stone stile to the right of the kink in the fence-line (75 yards to the right of an oak tree). In 200 metres we cross to the stile to the right of the road sign in **Galley Batch Lane**.

(21) Turn left (N) to the cross-roads in 50 metres. Turn right here (E), along **Pound Lane**, for 175 metres.

(22) Turn right across a stone stile opposite a field gate, and bear left in the field (SE), across to the concrete stile beside the left-hand conifers of **Oakhill Manor** in 200 metres. Cross into the parkland and then follow the path to the left (E) through a gate in 150 metres. We pass the **Old Farm** and **Coach House**, followed by the **Dower House**, to emerge beside **Grange House** in another 150 metres. This is **Zion Hill** and we turn right (S) to descend to the **High Street** in 200 metres.

In the 1890s, John Maitland Spencer built Hillylands - now known as Oakhill Manor - and incorporated masonry from a ruinous Georgian mansion known as Stoke House.

9 Cranmore & Doulting

Steam trains through quarrylands to a saint's shrine and tithe barn

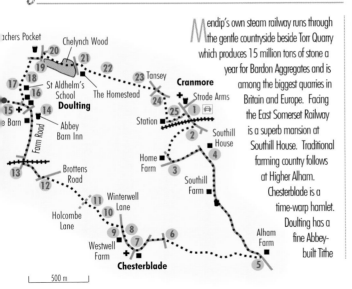

Mendip's own steam railway runs through the gentle countryside beside Torr Quarry which produces 15 million tons of stone a year for Bardon Aggregates and is among the biggest quarries in Britain and Europe. Facing the East Somerset Railway is a superb mansion at Southill House. Traditional farming country follows at Higher Alham. Chesterblade is a time-warp hamlet. Doulting has a fine Abbey-built Tithe

Level:
Length: 8 miles
Terrain: Usual muddy patches and occasional areas of undergrowth but no stiff climbs.
Park and start: At West Cranmore near the Strode Arms or Cranmore Railhead.
Start ref: ST 667 431 **Postcode:** BA4 4QJ
Public transport: Buses between Frome and Radstock.
Websites: www.cranmore-somerset.co.uk
www.eastsomersetrailway.com

Barn, mediaeval cross, and sacred spring at St Aldhelm's Well. Quarrylands new and old date back to Roman times with easily-carved limestone still being worked around Chelynch. Cranmore has characterful corners.

1 Set off southwards along the road from the **Strode Arms**, passing the entrance to the station yard, and cross the railway bridge in 150 metres. On the other side of the bridge, at a gateway in 100 metres, we turn right into the field (W) and then bear right to the corner below the Victorian buildings of **Cranmore Station** in 300 metres.

2 Now bear left (SW), across the field towards **Home Farm One**, to the right of the wood. Go through the gate into the next field and cross it diagonally to pass to the left of the farmhouse and walk up to the road in 600 metres.

3 Turn left (E) to pass **Home Farm Two** and follow the road to the junction beside the grounds of **Southill House** in 500 metres.

4 Turn right along this lane (SW), into the valley, to **Southill Farm** in 700 metres. Proceed to **Alham Farm** in 1,000 metres. This ancient collection of buildings includes a barn with a pigeon loft.

5 Turn right (W) on reaching the farmyard wall at the bottom

Southill House

East Somerset Railway, dating from 1858, was saved by wildlife artist David Shepherd who rescued locomotives from the scrap-yard and revived the line for steam working in 1973.

of the hill, into a stony double-hedged lane. This becomes a grassy green lane which emerges at a road junction in 1,500 metres.

6 Proceed straight ahead. The Iron Age fortifications of Small Down Camp ring the hillside across to our left. Turn left (SW) at the next junction in 225 metres and descend into the hamlet of **Chesterblade** in 300 metres. **St**

'Black Prince' 92203

Mary's is a simple single-cell church, surrounded by yew trees, beside the junction opposite Cypress House.

(7) Carry on up the hill along **Winterwell Lane** (N). Pass the pound, on the left, in 75 metres. Leave the hamlet at **Westwell Farm** and proceed for 250 metres towards the pylon line.

(8) Before reaching it, and also before coming to an ash tree and a barn, we turn left (NW) through a field gate. Then bear right, up to the gate into the next field in 100 metres. Turn left in this field, with the barn behind you, to follow the hedge uphill to the nearest pylon in 200 metres. Lamyatt Beacon, which had a Roman temple, is across to your left.

(9) Go through the gate to the left of the pylon and bear right, under the cables, diagonally down the slope to a stile to the left of the gate two-thirds along the lower hedgerow in 350 metres.

(10) Bear right in this field to a stone stile between the ash trees in 150 metres. Cross **Holcombe Lane** to the other side and follow the left-hand hedgerow straight ahead, up and over hill into the top corner in 250 metres.

(11) Here we go through the gate and proceed along the valley edge. Then bear right to hedgerow gates in 400 metres. The pylon line is now across to our left.

Doulting Tithe Barn

12 Turn left along **Brottens Road** (SW) and then right (NW) at the junction in 50 metres. We are heading downhill towards Doulting.

13 Turn right at the next junction in 400 metres, to cross the railway bridge (still authentically smoke-blackened) and pass **Brambleditch Cottage**. Continue straight ahead (N) along Farm Road which passes the **Tithe Barn** - built by Glastonbury Abbey estate - and **Abbey Barn Inn** in 750 metres.

14 Cross the main road, into the village street, and follow it straight ahead into **Church Lane** (W) to **St Aldhelm's Church** in 150 metres. The 23-feet high churchyard cross dates from the 15th century as is attributed to the penultimate Abbot of Glastonbury.

15 Turn right at the churchyard gate (N) into a gravel path between stone piers. This brings us to **Grailhaven** in 100 metres. Here we turn left, down the slope for a diversion to mediaeval **St Aldhelm's Well** in 150 metres. There is a trough in the front wall but the ancient stonework lies behind where a spring emerges through miniature arches beneath the sycamore trees.

16 Having turned around we walk uphill for 250 metres to **Rowan Cottage**, opposite Doulting Lodge, where we turn left into Beech Close. Then bear left in 25 metres, behind Rowan Cottage, straight ahead along an alleyway (N) behind houses and then **St Aldhelm's Primary School**, to the end of its compound in 300 metres.

17 Follow the hedgerow to a stone stile in 50 metres. Then follow a grassy terrace straight ahead, keeping the same hedge to your right for 300 metres, to the right-hand extremity of **Pitts Wood** at the end of the pasture.

18 Here we turn right and then left, across an architectural stile, to cross old quarrylands to a conventional stile to the left of the bungalows in 150 metres. A wooded quarry is now to our left as we proceed to a stone stile and the road in 75 metres.

19 Turn right (E), uphill to the junction at **Chelynch** in 150 metres. Here we turn left (N), towards the **Poacher's Pocket**, for 75 metres.

20 Now turn right (E), into a grassy strip beside **Chelynch Wood**. Keep this and a quarry to

St Aldhelm's Well

your right and cross restored quarry-lands to the hedgerow to the left of the cottage in 600 metres.

21 Cross **Farrington Lane** to the grass strip behind the **Homestead** and then turn right across a stile, beside the gate, in 20 metres. Bear left across the paddock (SE), to a stone stile midway along the hedgerow, in 100 metres. Then cross to the next stile in 50 metres. Ditto across the following pasture for another 50 metres. Follow the old wall straight ahead for 40 metres in the final paddock.

22 Now follow the left-hand hedgerow for 300 metres as the sound of main road traffic intrudes from the right. From the stile in the

corner we cross a field, aiming for the left-hand end of the pylon line, to a stile with the main road behind it. Cranmore Tower, a Victorian folly, is across to our left. Bear left in the following field, in 250 metres, towards a point to the left of the hedge beside the main road at **Tansey**.

23 Cross a stile in 400 metres and bear right beside the cricket pitch for 100 metres. This brings us to a stile beside the bus shelter where we turn right (S) to the cross-roads in 20 metres. Cross the main road.

24 Walk along **Piers Road** for 30 metres and then turn right, opposite the lodge, across a stile into the field. Proceed to a stile in 200 metres, just to the left of the

bungalow beside Cranmore Station. Exit from this field in another 200 metres, in the corner, between the bungalow and the house. Then turn left, through the trees, to the drive in 20 metres.

25 Turn left (E) to the sidings and **Signal Box**, in 50 metres, and pass **Cranmore Station** along the access road to the entrance to the car-park in 250 metres. **Whistle Stop Tea Shop** faces us and just around the corner, opposite the village duck-pond, is the **Strode Arms**.

Southill House was the elegant Georgian seat of the Strode family, followed by the Huntley-Spencers and Poyntz-Wrights.

10 Mells & Great Elm

Literary and political associations abound in a landscape of old and new mineral industries

Mells Manor was built by Little Jack Horner of nursery rhyme fame. He sat in his corner in the office of Thomas Cromwell, Earl of Essex, as a clerk, while his master dismembered the monasteries for

Level: 🥾
Length: 6 miles
Terrain: Though they pass through robust countryside, the paths are relatively unchallenging.
Park and start: At **Mells**, in **Selwood Street**, in the vicinity of the 18th-century **Talbot Inn**.
Start ref: ST 727 493 **Postcode:** BA11 3PN
Public transport: Buses from Shepton Mallet to Frome.
Websites: www.somerset.gov.uk/her/details
www.uk.villages.co.uk

King Henry VIII. Mells was his plum, picked from the pile of deeds and rolls that accumulated around them, in the 1530s. The Mells place-name derives from 'Mulle' for mill.

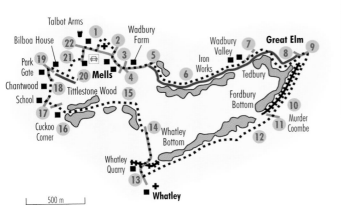

Talbot Arms
Bilboa House
Park Gate
Chantwood
School
Cuckoo Corner
Mells
Tittlestone Wood
Wadbury Farm
Wadbury Valley
Iron Works
Great Elm
Tedbury
Fordbury Bottom
Murder Coombe
Whatley Bottom
Whatley Quarry
Whatley

500 m

1 Set off along **New Street** - new in 1490 - to **St Andrew's Church** (N) in 100 metres. Continue straight ahead through the churchyard - along the yew avenue - to a gate in the wall in another 200 metres.

2 Turn right (SE) in **Fairfield**, passing the end of the churchyard in 50 metres, into the corner of the field beside the houses in 200 metres. Turn right (SSW) on joining the road and walk down to a second junction, beside the war memorial, in 50 metres.

3 Turn left (SE), downhill, between **Ivy Cottage** and **Clothiers**. Continue straight ahead to the Post Office in 200 metres. The Mark Horner memorial shelter is to your right.

4 Our onward route is ahead for a few paces, into the wide junction, where we take the second road on the left (E). This passes **Wadbury Farm**.

The Mells masterpiece is a life-size equestrian statue by Alfred Munnings, in the church chancel, on a plinth by Edwin Lutyens, to commemorate Lieutenant Edward Horner of the Queen Mary's Own Hussars who fell in Picardy on 21 November 1917.

Talbot Arms

THE TALBOT
FREE HOUSE

5 On approaching the bend in 350 metres we turn right (SE) into a tarred bridleway. This carried a horse-drawn tramway into **Wadbury Valley**. The remains of **Fussell's Ironworks** begin at a mill leat. In 800 metres, after the cascade coming out of the rocks, we bear left on approaching the main collection of derelict buildings a kiln.

6 Keep these and their long wall to your right. We emerge in a deep-cut section of the wooded ravine and follow the **Mells Stream** (NE). In 400 metres we come to a drive below clifftop houses and their enviable rock-gardens. Then in 150 metres we bear right, at the foot of the hill, and follow a public path across the grass. Keep the stream to your right.

7 In 400 metres we come to a footbridge. Cross it and bear left (SE) on the other side. We now keep the stream to our left and the Iron Age slopes of rocky **Tedbury** on the right.

8 On reaching **Great Elm** in 400 metres we come to a tributary and turn right and then to cross it, at a footbridge, beside a railway cutting. Bear left (NE) for 100 metres to gates beside a road.

9 Turn right - after admiring the river-sized pool beside the bridge - and follow the road up the hill for 100 metres. Then turn

Mells Manor and Church

61

right (SE), up into the trees, and turn right again (SW) in 40 metres. Keep the fields to your left as you skirt the top side of the wooded valley.

10 After 100 metres the railway appears to the right, deep down in **Fordbury Bottom**. In 500 metres we come to the road at **Murder Combe**.

11 Turn left (E), uphill for 40 metres, and then right (SW). Follow the hedgerow to the end of the field in 400 metres. Then turn right into a double-hedged track.

12 Turn left (SW) on reaching the wood in 150 metres, over a stile, into the next field. We are heading towards Whatley church spire and

Manor Farm. The quarries of **Whatley Bottom** are down to your right, screened by trees, and we continue to the far end of this belt of woodland.

13 Here, in 1,250 metres, we descend steps to a road. Turn right (N), away from Whatley village,

and use the pavement or verge, making sure you walk towards oncoming traffic when neither is available. Listen for lorries as you approach and pass **Whatley Quarry** railhead.

14 In 500 metres, on the slope shortly after the second quarry entrance - where blasting times are given on a notice board - we turn left (NW) across a stile in the hedgerow. Our onward route is now between the quarry bund and the roadside hedge.

(15) In 400 metres we continue around the corner (W). Bear left (WSW) in 250 metres to follow electricity cables, across rough pasture. Mells, with its Manor House and church tower, is across to the right. Continue to the far end of **Tittlestone Wood** which is also to our right.

(16) Here, on approaching an old orchard in 600 metres, we cross a stile in the fence-line to the right of another stile which is set in a stone wall. The path across our wooden stile leads (NW) to a stone

stile at **Cuckoo Corner** in 100 metres.

(17) Bear left, downhill, to the road above **Gunder Well** in 175 metres. Here we turn left and then right, on **Mells Green**, and walk across it to **Mells School** in 150 metres.

(18) Now turn right (N), passing **Chantwood**, down the grassy slope beside the road to the far end of the common land beside a tri-angle of roadside grass at **Mells Park Gate** in 300 metres.

(19) Cross the main road on the bend, along the drive to

Fussell's Ironworks

Whatley Quarry

mediaeval **Bilboa House** which seems to grow out of an old quarry. Beside it the drive turns right (SE), becoming **Doctor's Walk**, which we follow to the **Reading Room** in the former Bell Inn, beside the mill leat in 250 metres.

20 Turn left (NE) immediately after this 18th-century house, up the slope to the thatched cottage at the end of **Rashwood Lane** in 100 metres. From here we proceed straight ahead, across a stone stile, into the recreation ground. Follow the right-hand hedge (NE) to the thatched buildings of **Garston Gate** in 200 metres. Cross stiles, or go through the gate, to join **Gay Street** in 50 metres.

21 Turn left (N), downhill, beside the tall wall of the **Rectory** grounds, to the road junction in 150 metres.

22 Turn right (E), beside Talbot hound mascots of the Horner family whose descendants are still in residence, at the entrance to the **Manor House**. Return along **Selwood Street** to the **Talbot Arms** in 200 metres.

The alphabet put the name of Prime Minister's son Raymond Asquith first on the village war memorial: 'We died in a strange land facing the dark cloud of war, and this stone is raised to us in the home of our delight.'

Fussell's Ironworks, founded by James Fussell (1748-1832), extended half a mile along Wadbury Valley.